DOCKER

Docker Guide
for Production Environment

**(Docker Containers, Docker
Orchestration, Docker Deployment
Tools, Fig, Drone, Wrapdocker Tools,
Docker Security)**

By Matthew Gimson

Table of Contents

Disclaimer

While all attempts have been made to verify the information provided in this book, the author does assume any responsibility for errors, omissions, or contrary interpretations of the subject matter contained within. **The information provided in this book is for educational and entertainment purposes only. The reader is responsible for his or her own actions and the author does not accept any responsibilities for any liabilities or damages, real or perceived, resulting from the use of this information.**

The trademarks that are used are without any consent, and the publication of the trademark is without permission or backing by the trademark owner. All trademarks and brands within this book are for clarifying purposes only and are the owned by the owners themselves, not affiliated with this document.

Introduction

The Docker is very important software. In the first part of this book, we explored most of its basic details. My hope is that you have read the first part of this book. This will help you to learn and understand the contents of this book easier and faster. However, there are more complex and important aspects of the Docker which you still need to know. These are the topics discussed in this book. Most of the features of the Docker which are important for use in the production environments have been explored in detail.

For instance, in most production environments, Linux is used as the operating system. This is why you need to know to deploy the Docker in these environments. This will be discussed in this book. Docker security is also very important. This will also be explored in this book. Orchestration of the Docker needs to be known well. It has also been discussed in this book. The internal composition and processes of the Docker need to be understood well. This book will help you in that. You also need to know how to configure the Docker for networking.

Chapter 1- Definition

From the first part of this book, you learned what the Docker is, and where and how it is used. You are now aware that it is an open-source project for deployment of software in distributed environments. You also learned of how it provides or implements the concept of virtualization, as only the details which are important to the users are made accessible to them. Installation of the Docker was also explored. We said that it relies on features which are related to Linux.

This is why we explored the installation of the Docker in Mac OS X and Windows operating systems. It cannot be installed natively on these operating systems. We used a software called *"Boot2Docker"* so as to install the Docker in these operating systems. However, this is different in Linux as we are going to see in the next topics. We do not use the Boot2Docker to install the Docker in Linux. The Docker images and containers were explored, but only shallowly. In this book, we will explore this in depth.

The whalesay image was discussed. You are aware of how to find it from the Docker hub, download it, and use it on your machine. Building of Docker images was also explored. You should be in a position to create your own Docker image and use it on your machine. You can also upload to the public Docker hub where others will find and download it for their own use. You should also be able to create a Docker repository and account. This can either be a private or a public account. Pulling and tagging of images in the Docker hub was discussed, so you should be in a position to perform these tasks. This shows how the first part of this book is important. Familiarize yourself with the basics of the Docker by reading the first part, and you will find it easy to understand this second part.

Chapter 2- Deployment and testing of Docker-based Linux containers

Docker features are solely based on Linux operating system. This is why it is natively installed on this operating system. Unlike in other operating systems such as the Windows and Mac OS X, we do not have to use the Boot2Docker in this case. It is also easy for us to install the Docker on any distribution of Linux. In this chapter, we will explore the installation and testing of the Docker on various distributions of Linux. However, for each distribution of Linux, there some versions which support the Docker, while others do not. Most production environments use the Linux operating system, so there is a need for you to install the Docker in Linux.

Installation of Docker in Ubuntu

The following versions of Ubuntu Linux support the Docker:

- Ubuntu Precise 12.04 (LTS)

- Ubuntu Trusty 14.04 (LTS)

- Ubuntu Saucy 13.10

In this case, make sure that you download the latest version of the Docker before installing it.

Requirements

Regardless of the version of the Ubuntu Linux you are running on your system, the Docker requires you to choose a 64-bit installation. The minimum version of the Ubuntu kernel supported by the Docker is 3.10. Any other version newer than this can be supported by the Docker.

Kernels versions lower than 3.10 are known for data loss and their lack of features which are necessary for us to run the Docker containers. You should determine the version of the kernel which is running on your system. Just open the Ubuntu terminal and run the following command:

uname –r

In my case, I get the following output from the command:

```
$ uname -r
3.11.0-15-generic
```

The version of my kernel is greater than 3.10 as shown in the figure above. This shows that I can safely install the Docker on my system and all will be well.

If you are running Ubuntu Trusty 14.04 on your machine, then you are better off, as there are no prerequisites needed before installing the Docker. However, if you are running Ubuntu precise 12.04 (LTS) on your system, then a kernel version of not less than 13.13 will be needed. If this requirement has not been met, you can choose to upgrade the package.

Upgrading the package

Now that your kernel version is lower than what is needed, you have to upgrade it to a higher version. To do this, just follow the steps given below:

1. Login to your Ubuntu host and then open the terminal.

2. Run the following command so as to update the package manager:

```
$ sudo apt-get update
```

If prompted to enter the *"sudo"* password, do so. This can be different from the normal password you used to log into the system.

3. You should now install the optional and the additional packages by use of the following command:

```
$ sudo apt-get install linux-image-generic-lts-trusty
```

The packages to be installed will depend the version of Ubuntu that you are using.

4. Once done, run the following command so as to reboot the host:

```
$ sudo reboot
```

5. Once the system has rebooted, you can then start to install the Docker.

The Installation Process

Now that you have all of the needed prerequisites, you can install the Docker. This can be done by following the steps given below:

1. Start the machine running Ubuntu and then login as the Sudo user.

2. Verify whether the *"wget"* has been installed on your system or not. Run the following command:

```
$ which wget
```

If it is not installed, update the package manager as follows before installing it:

```
$ sudo apt-get update
```

You can then install it as follows:

```
$ sudo apt-get install wget
```

3. Use the following command so as to download the latest package of the Docker.

```
$ wget -qO- https://get.docker.com/ | sh
```

If prompted to provide the sudo password, do so. Docker together with its dependencies will be downloaded and installed on your system. After a while, the process will be completed.

4. You can then verify whether the installation was successful or not by using the following command:

```
$ sudo docker run hello-world
```

With the above command, a test image will be downloaded and then run on the container. A message written *"Hello from Docker"* should be printed on the terminal if the installation was successful. Otherwise, repeat the installation process.

Docker Installation in Oracle Linux

This version of Linux is a commercial one and mostly used in production environments. People who use this distribution of Linux usually subscribe with payment of a fee, so as to receive the updates. However, you do not need an active subscription to install the Docker on this distribution of Linux. If your Oracle Linux has an active subscription, visit ULN (Unbreakable Linux Network) and you will find both *"ol7_x86_64_addons"* and *"ol6_x86_64_addons"* channels of the Docker, which you can download and use on your system.

For the users of Oracle Linux whose subscription is not active, visit the same site and you will find "*ol7_addons*" or "*ol6_addons*", which are Docker repositories. For the Docker to work on Oracle Linux, the version of the kernel should not be less than 3. This applies to both Oracle Linux 6 and 7.

However, since there are some limitations to this, the Docker can only run on either 32 or 64 bit versions of this.

Before beginning to install the Docker on your Oracle Linux machine, you have to enable the addons channel. This can be done via the Unbreakable Linux Network (ULN).

The Installation Process

1. Before beginning this process, make sure that you have the appropriate repository or addons channel enabled on your system.

2. After this, you can use the "*yum*" command which will help you to install the Docker package. This is shown below:

```
$ sudo yum install docker
```

Once you run the above command, the Docker together with its dependencies will be installed on your machine. It will then be ready for use.

Starting the Docker

Now that the Docker has been installed on your system, the Docker daemon can be started. This can be done as follows:

1. If you are using Oracle Linux 6, run the following command:

```
$ sudo service docker start
```

2. If you are using Oracle Linux 7, run the following command:

```
$ sudo systemctl start docker.service
```

For some users, your aim is for the Docker to be started once the system boots. This is possible and it can be done as follows:

1. If you are using Oracle Linux 6, run the following command:

```
$ sudo chkconfig docker on
```

2. If you are using Oracle Linux 7, run the following command:

```
$ sudo systemctl enable docker.service
```

You will then be done and ready to start using the Docker.

How to use the btrfs storage engine

This storage engine is supported by the Docker running on either the Oracle Linux 6 or 7. It is good for you to enable the support for this, but before doing so, make sure that the "/var/lib/docker" has been stored in a file system which is based on btrsf.

For you to enable the support for btrfs in Oracle Linux, follow the steps given below:

1. Begin checking on whether the "/var/lib/docker" is on a file system which is based on btrfs. If this is not the case, then make it so.

2. Open the file "/etc/sysconfig/docker". Identify the field "OTHER_ARGS" and then add "-s btrfs" to it.

3. You can the restart the Docker daemon.

Uninstallation of the Docker

Once you are done with your tasks, you can choose to uninstall the Docker from your machine. To do this, use the following command:

```
$ sudo yum -y remove docker
```

The command will uninstall the Docker package from your computer. However, for the case of volumes, images, containers and configuration files which have been created by the user, they will not be removed from the system by the above command. If you need to do this, then use the command given below:

```
$ rm -rf /var/lib/docker
```

However, the configuration files which have been created by the user will not be deleted by using this command. To delete them, then you have to do it manually. You now know the various aspects of the Docker running on Oracle Linux 6 or 7, ranging from its installation to uninstallation.

Installation of Docker in Red Hat Enterprise Linux

The following versions of Red Hat Linux support the Docker:

- Red Hat Enterprise Linux 7

- Red Hat Enterprise Linux 6.6 or later

This section will guide you on how to use Docker managed release packages and the Installation mechanisms, to install the Docker on Red Hat Enterprise Linux. However, it will be best for you to download the latest release of the Docker.

Requirements

Regardless the version of Red Hat enterprise Linux that you are using on your system, the Docker will require a 64-bit installation. The minimum version of the kernel which can be supported is 3.10, so ensure that you have this or a newer version. However, if you are using Red Hat version 6.6, the kernel version should be 2.6.32-431 or higher.

If you do not know the version of the kernel on your machine, open the terminal and then run the command "*uname –r*". This is shown in the figure below:

```
$ uname -r
3.10.0-229.el7.x86_64
```

You also need to update your system fully. There is a possibility that errors with the kernel will arise during the installation process. This is why you need to fully patch the system.

The Installation process

For all version of Red Hat Linux, the installation procedure is the same. However, what differs is the package that is to be installed. To install the Docker on this distribution of Linux, follow the following steps:

1. Start the computer and then login as a sudo user.

2. In the current directory, download the Docker package by use of the command given below:

   curl -O -sSL

   http://get.docker.com/docker/1.7.0/rpms/cent os-6/RPMS/x86_64/docker-engine-1.7.0-0.1.el6.x86_64.rpm

3. Once the package has been downloaded, you can use the *"yum"* command to install it onto your system. The following command can be used for this purpose:

   sudo yum localinstall --nogpgcheck docker-engine-1.7.0-0.1.el6.x86_64.rpm

4. You can then use the following command to start the Docker daemon:

```
$ sudo service docker start
```

5. Since you are done with the installation process, you can now verify whether it was successful or not. The following command can be used:

```
$ sudo docker run hello-world
```

The above command will download and then run the test image from the Docker Hub. It will run verbally and you will see the following text on the terminal:

```
Unable to find image 'hello-world:latest' locally
latest: Pulling from hello-world
a8219747be10: Pull complete
91c95931e552: Already exists
hello-world:latest: The image you are pulling has been verifi
Digest: sha256:aa03e5d0d5553b4c3473e89c8619cf79df368babd18681
Status: Downloaded newer image for hello-world:latest
Hello from Docker.
This message shows that your installation appears to be worki
```

Once you see the *"Hello from Docker"* message shown in the above figure, you know the installation process was successul. You can then start using the Docker for other purposes.

Creation of a Docker Group

The binding of the docker daemon is done to a UNIX socket rather than to a TCP port. This socket is owned by the *"root"* user. For other users of the system to access it, they must use the *"sudo"* command. This shows that the daemon for the Docker runs as the root user.

However, we need to avoid the use of this *"sudo"* command. This can only be done by creation of a group named *"docker"*. We can then add the users to this group and they will not have to use the *"sudo"* keyword in their Docker commands. With this, once the Docker daemon is started, The Docker just makes the UNIX socket readable and writable to the users added to the *"docker"* group. However, you should be careful while creating this group, since the users added to it will be like the *"root"* user.

To do this, follow the steps given below:

1. Login into the computer as a *"sudo"* or the *"root"* user.

2. Create a group named *"docker"* and then add your user to it. The syntax for this is given below:

sudo usermod -aG docker username

Simply log out of the system and then log in again. You will then be running or logged into the system with the sufficient privileges.

3. You can then verify whether you succeeded. To do this, just run any of the Docker commands without the use of the *"sudo"* keyword and check to see if it works. This is shown below:

```
$ docker run hello-world
```

In my case, I got the *"Hello from Docker"* message meaning that I was successful.

```
Status: Downloaded newer image for hello-world:latest
Hello from Docker.
This message shows that your installation appears to be worl
```

In Red Hat Linux, it is possible for the Docker daemon to automatically start once the computer is booted. This can be set by running the following command on the terminal:

```
$ sudo chkconfig docker on
```

Uninstallation

You might need to uninstall the Docker from your Red Hat enterprise Linux OS. This is usually the case after one is done, or completes the task they were performing with the Docker. This can be done by the use of the *"yum"* command as shown below:

1. Begin by listing, to learn what kind of package you have installed on your computer. Use the following command for that purpose:

   ```
   $ yum list installed | grep docker
   ```

   In my system I get the following, showing the package which I have installed:

```
yum list installed | grep docker
docker-engine.x86_64                1.7.0-0.1.el6
```

2. The package can then be removed. This can be done by use of the following command:

```
$ sudo yum -y remove docker-engine.x86_64
```

The command will remove the package from your computer. However, volumes, containers, images and configuration files created by the user, will not be removed by use of the above command.

3. If you need to delete the above mentioned elements, that is, volumes, containers and images, then use the following command:

```
$ rm -rf /var/lib/docker
```

However, the above command will not delete the configuration files which were created by the user.

4. You can then locate and delete the configuration files which were created by the user. The deletion should be done manually.

Installation of the Docker in SUSE Linux Enterprise and OpenSUSE

For the users of SUSE Linux Enterprise 12 or later, you are lucky as these support the use of the Docker. However, the limitation associated with the Docker makes it able to run on a 64 bit architecture only. To install the Docker on this OS, follow the steps given below:

1. Install the package by running the following command:

```
$ sudo zypper in docker
```

2. Once the installation process completes, the Docker daemon can be started by use of the following command:

```
$ sudo systemctl start docker
```

3. You might also want the Docker to start automatically once the computer boots up. To set this up, use the following command:

```
$ sudo systemctl enable docker
```

A new group named *"docker"* will be created by the
Docker package. For the users, with the exception of the
"root" user, they should be added to this group so that
they can interact with the Docker daemon. To add users
to the group, just use the following command:

sudo /usr/sbin/usermod -a -G docker <name>

4. To perform a verification or a check on whether
everything ran correctly, use the following command:

```
$ sudo docker run --rm -i -t opensuse /bin/bash
```

With the above command, the OpenSuse image will be downloaded onto your system and then the *"bash"* will be started in the container. If you need to exit this, just type the command *"exit"* on the *"bash"*. You might also need the containers to be able to access the external network. For this, you have to enable the rule *"net.ipv4.ip_forward"*. YaST can be used for this purpose. Just navigate to *"Network Devices -> Network Settings -> Routing"*.

Find the checkbox written *"Enable IPv4 Forwarding"* and then enable it. However, if the *"Network Manager"* is responsible for handling the network, it will be hard for you to change this. In that case, you have to open the file *"/etc/sysconfig/SuSEfirewall2"* and make sure that the flag *"FW_ROUTE"* has been set to *"yes"*. This is shown below:

```
FW_ROUTE="yes"
```

Installation of the Docker in OpenSUSE

OpenSUSE 12.3 and later supports the use of the Docker. However, only the 64-bit architecture of this is supported. For the case of OpenSUSE 12.3 and OpenSUSE 13.1, a virtualization repository from OBS must be installed before we can install the Docker package. The reason behind this is that the Docker is not one of the official repositories for these versions of OpenSUSE.

The virtualization repository can be added by running the following command:

sudo zypper ar -f http://download.opensuse.org/repositories/Virtualiz ation/openSUSE_12.3/ Virtualization

This can also be achieved by running the following command:

sudo zypper ar -f http://download.opensuse.org/repositories/Virtualiz ation/openSUSE_13.1/ Virtualization

The Uninstallation process

If you need to uninstall the Docker package, then run the following command:

```
$ sudo zypper rm docker
```

However, the above command will not remove containers, images, volumes and configuration files created by the user. These can be removed by running the following command:

```
$ rm -rf /var/lib/docker
```

In the case of the configuration files created by the user, they have to be manually removed from your computer.

Chapter 3- Deeper understanding of Containers composition and internal processes

In the Docker, the client-server is used. This is a kind of architecture in which the client sends a request to the server and then the server relays a response to it.

Docker client

This is the first part of the Docker. It does not directly access or communicate to the Docker server. There is an intermediary between the two called the *"Docker daemon"*, which we will explore later.

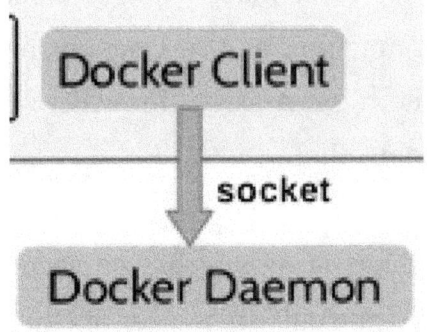

To run these components, you can choose to do it on the same machine or on different machines. As shown in the above figure, communication between the Docker client and the Docker daemon is node via a socket. A Restful API can also be used instead of the sockets.

Docker Daemon

The Docker users will not directly interact with the Docker daemon. They must perform interactions with the Docker client discussed above.

This will then relay their requests to the Docker daemon. It directly runs on the Host machine. The Docker client can be run on the same machine as the Docker daemon or you can choose to run them separately, in which case a means of connection will be needed.

The above discussion is about the external structure of the Docker. But the internal structure of the Docker is very important, as it is the one which gets the work done. This is where the real processing of the users' data is done.

The internal structure of the Docker is made up of the following components:

- Docker images

- Docker registries

- Docker containers

The Docker Images

Docker images are read-only. The Docker container is made up of Docker images. It is easy for us to create new Docker images on our own as we discussed in the first part of this book. These are uploaded to the Docker hub where other people can access and download them for their own use. The images are the major components of the Docker.

Docker Registries

These are used for the purpose of holding images. They act as stores, and they can be either private or public. If public, the images you upload will be accessible and downloadable by others for their use. If private, this will not be the case. The Docker Hub, which we discussed in the first part of this book, is an example of the public Docker registry.

They form the distribution component for the Docker.

Docker Containers

These can be compared to directories at the operating system level. Just like the directories, the container is used for holding everything which is necessary for the Docker to run. To create a Docker container, we use the Docker image. They form the component of the Docker which can be started, stopped and deleted.

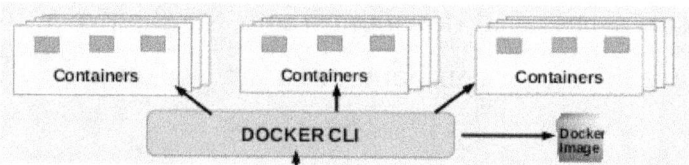

The functionality of a Docker image

Now that you are aware of most components of the Docker, you need to understand how they work in more depth.

A Docker image is made up of multiple layers. To combine these layers into one, the Docker uses the union file system. With this kind of file system, all the images, regardless of their type, are joined together into one. These layers explain the lightweight nature of the Docker. It is possible for you to update the Docker image that you are using. When you do this, a new layer is added to the already existing layers of the Docker image.

Notice a new layer has been added or an existing one has been updated, rather than restructuring the whole system, like what we have in the Virtual Machine. This is why it is easy for us to distribute the Docker images. Each of the Docker images has a base image from which it is built. We use instructions to build these. A single instruction adds a new layer to the image and the cycle continues until we have our complete and fully functional image.

A file named "*Dockerfile*" is used for storage of these instructions. Whenever you request an instruction, this file is read by the Docker, the instruction is executed and then the final result is returned to you.

The functionality of the Docker container

The Docker container is made up of the OS (operating system), meta-data and files added by the user. As we said earlier, we use an image to build a container. The image tells the container what it should hold, the process to run when it is started and other types of information about the configuration. Note that the image is read-only. Whenever the container is run from the image, a read-write layer will be added on top of the image allowing your application to run.

After running the container?

The Docker container is run via the API or by use of Docker binaries. The Docker client is responsible for instructing the Docker daemon to launch the container. Consider the command shown below:

```
$ docker run -i -t ubuntu /bin/bash
```

The following sequence of events takes place after running the above command:

1. The *"Ubuntu"* image is pulled- the Docker begins by checking for the presence of the image in the local system. If it is not available, it is pulled from the Docker. However, there is no pulling if the image is found to exist locally.

2. A new container is created- once the image is obtained, it is used for creation of a new container.

3. Mounting of a read-write layer and allocation of a file system- creation of the container is done in the file system and a read-write layer is added to the image.

4. Allocation of an interface for the network/bridge- this is responsible for allowing the Docker container to communicate with the local host.

5. IP address set up- an IP address is found from the pool and then attached.

6. Execution of the specified process- at this stage, the application is executed.

7. Capturing and provision of application output- the standard input is connected and then logged. Any errors and outputs are provided to you.

After the above final step, you can perform any other tasks that you need with your Docker.

Chapter 4- Docker Deployment Tools

Docker is very important for apps development. The developer can easily do their job without the need to worry about the configuration of the computers for other developers.

However, the developers usually experience problems while trying to deploy their apps in a production environment. In this chapter, you will be guided on how to deploy your Rails app in a production environment.

The process

Remember the following commands, which we used for starting and linking together of our containers.

```
$ docker run -d --name database test/postgres
```

The above command was used for starting of the container.

```
$ docker run -i -t --name web --link database:database -p 45000:80
```

The above command will link the containers together.

For most people, keeping the above two commands is a problem. Note the use of the flags, which most people find it difficult to memorize. However, this problem can be solved by use of *"Fig"*.

FIG

Some Dockerfiles will only describe how one can build an individual container. However, with Fig, the entire infrastructure of the container can be specified. With this, a single YAML file is used for addition of volumes, linking of containers and opening of ports. Consider the following code for the *"fig.yml"* file:

```yaml
web:

build: .

ports:

- "80:80"

links:

- database

database:

image: postgres

ports:

- "5432"

volumes:

- /etc/postgresql

- /var/log/postgresql

- /var/lib/postgresql
```

In the above figure, we have two containers, that is, "*web*" and "*database*". We need to join them together. The container "*web*" will be built from the Dockerfile and in the current directory. After exposing the port number 80, it is then linked to the "*database*" container. The image "*postgressSQL*" will be obtained by the "*database*" container from the Docker Hub and then the port 5432 will be exposed to the other containers. The containers can be built and started by use of the following commands:

```
$ fig build

$ fig up -d
```

The first command is for building while the second one is for starting the build container. The linked container, which is the "*database*", container, should be started first. This is because we do not want the "*web*" to be started without using the database. With the "*-d*" flag, the Fig will run in the background.

Deployment

The Docker container can now be started, but the question how to make it work in a production server. If both the Fig and the container have been installed, we need only clone the remote repository and then execute the previous g=fig commands, which will start up our containers. Note that although Fig is good for the purpose of starting containers, it is not good for restarting them. During recreation of the containers, there will be none available for the purpose of servicing requests. This is why we should directly use the Docker commands and then use Nginx for balancing the requests. Consider the figure given below:

```
web:

build: .

ports:

- "8080:80"

links:

- db

...
```

We have changed the ports exposed to the web container. At this point, it is not running on port number 80. We need the Nginx to listen at that port. When Fig is started for the first time, the requests at port 8080 will be handled by the *"web"* container. For the configuration of Nginx, the balance should be done between ports 8080 and 8081. The default site configuration for the Nginx should be as follows:

```
upstream docker {

server 127.0.0.1:8080;

server 127.0.0.1:8081;

}

server {

listen 80;

location / {

proxy_pass http://docker;

}

}
```

Once the Nginx is started, it will immediately begin to balance requests between the ports 8080 and 8081. However, one of these ports might have failed. In this case, no requests will be sent to it until it has been backed up. We can then use Git to pull our remote changes and then the following command should be used for starting a new container:

```
$ docker run -d --name web1 --link cjournal_databaseb_1:database -p 8081:80 cjournal_web:latest
```

Now that we are sure that the requests are being served, we can stop the other container. It is highly recommended at this stage to use the Docker command rather than the Fig, since the latter can negatively affect the container "*database*" which is already running.

With this configuration, any number of containers can be arbitrarily started, but the name and the host port need to be changed while updating the configuration of Nginx.

Use of Drone to build and deploy Docker images

We have an application which can be deployed as a Docker container. We also have a drone server which is functioning well.

Configuring the application for Drone

We need to begin by connecting the repository of the app to a drone server which is working effectively. Consider the figure given below:

```
/myrepository

|

|---- .drone.yml (required)

|

|---- /.drone (optional)

| |

| |---- build.sh

| |---- deploy.sh

|

|---- CODE..
```

By default, the "*/.drone*" will be used for storage of the drone resources. The file "*.drone.yml*" will have the following:

```
image: http://the-docker-registry/the-docker-image.version

script:

- ./.drone/build.sh

deploy:

bash:

script:

- ./drone/deploy.sh

notify:

email:

recipients:

- name@domain.com
```

Now let us move in a step-by-step procedure:

1. Begin by specifying the build image. This is shown below:

```
image: http://the-docker-registry/the-docker-image.version
```

The pre-built images for drone are available when demanded, having common build tools. It is also possible for you to specify your own. In this case, we will use a custom image.

2. Show the build commands which are available. This is shown below:

```
script:

    - ./.drone/build.sh
```

What we have done is forward to a bash script. You will understand this further later.

3. Show the deployment commands:

```
deploy:

bash:

script:

- ./drone/deploy.sh
```

Note that in drone, there are numerous deployment options but in this case, we have used *"deploy → bash → script"*.

4. Use an email to notify the people:

```
email:

recipients:

- name@domain.com
```

Building the Docker image

In this case, a Docker container running in Drone host forms our environment. However, we need a Docker image to be the output of the process running inside the build container. This is why we should have an instance of the Docker running inside.

The Docker should be running along side some other build tools. The following code might need to be added to the Dockerfile of the build container:

```
# install docker

RUN apt-get install -y apparmor

RUN curl -s https://get.docker.io/ubuntu/ | sudo sh
```

If we add the scrip "*init*" to our build container, then we can be in a position to start the Docker daemon. We can also start it by ourselves in the file "*build.sh*".

Using Wrapdocker

It is difficult for us to run a Docker inside another Docker. However, a solution to this has been provided in which we are able to bash script wrapper for the purpose of starting an instance of the Docker running inside. The following are the tasks accomplished by wrapdocker:

1. Ensures a correct mounting of the *"cgroups"*.

2. Ensures that extraneous *"file descriptors"* are closed.

3. Ensures that the Docker is started at the correct port.

We can then modify the Dockerfile of our build container to use the wrapdocker. This is shown below:

```
# install docker

RUN apt-get install -y apparmor

RUN curl -s https://get.docker.io/ubuntu/ | sudo sh

ADD wrapdocker /usr/local/bin/wrapdocker

RUN chmod +x /usr/local/bin/wrapdocker
```

What we have done in the above file is added two lines:

```
ADD wrapdocker /usr/local/bin/wrapdocker
```

The above line is responsible for adding a local copy of the wrapdocker into our build container. However, it is also possible for you to use the "*wget*" so as to obtain it from either Dropbox or Github.

```
RUN chmod +x /usr/local/bin/wrapdocker
```

The above command is responsible for making the wrapdocker executable. However, this can also be enabled by changing some permissions on the wrapdocker file.

The privileged flag

This is the outer support. When this is enabled on a particular container and it is run, it will be in a position to identify the resources of other hosts and then try to utilize them. Some of these resources are necessary for the Docker to run. The outer container in this case is just a build environment, which is controlled by Drone and responsible for exposing the privileged option. This will be done in the Drone web UI.

Just open the page for your repository and then open "Settings". Click on the "Admin-only Settings" and then enable the checkbox "Enable Privileged Builds". This is shown in the figure below:

☑ Enable Build Hooks

☑ Enable Pull Hooks

☑ Private

Admin-only settings.

☑ Enable Privileged Builds

The build script

We now need to write our actual build script. At this point, our Docker can be successfully ran inside a Docker container. The build script, that is *"build.sh",* should be as follows:

```
#!/bin/bash
set -e
cd /var/cache/drone/src/path/to/app
# [tests should be passed here]
wrapdocker &
sleep 10
docker build -t docker-registry/image-name .
docker push docker-registry/image-name
```

Let us explore the above code in details.

```
set -e
```

With the above code, we will be in a position to exit in case a failure occurs. A failure is represented by a non-zero code. If this is the case, Drone is informed and then it will stop or terminate the build process. If this was not the case, then the build would now undergo some tests.

/var/cache/drone/src/path/to/app

The above code is responsible for coping the source to the above location. We have then made it the working directory by use of the following command:

```
cd /var/cache/drone/src/path/to/app
```

We have then specified the tests which are to be carried out. It is after this that we start the Docker by using the following command:

```
wrapdocker &
```

```
sleep 10
```

We then build and push the Docker image. We use the following commands for that purpose:

```
docker build -t docker-registry/image-name .
```

The above command is for building the Docker image.

```
docker push docker-registry/image-name
```

The above command will push the image to the Docker registry, which is the Docker Hub. Our next step is to stop the Docker from execution. To do this, we can append *"service docker stop"* to the script *"build.sh"*. However, this fails with some setups. This can be used by use of the following alternative:

```
start-stop-daemon --stop --pidfile "/var/run/docker.pid"
```

However, in my case, I have kept the above command in its own file and I will name it after the *"build.sh"* script. This is shown below:

```
#!/bin/bash

start-stop-daemon --stop --pidfile "/var/run/docker.pid"
```

Deploying the Docker Image

To manually deploy a Docker app in a simple manner, we only have to log into the production machine. We can then *"docker pull"* and *"docker run"* the container.

The Deployment script

You are aware of the following:

```
#!/bin/bash
set -e
docker pull docker-registry/image-name:latest
docker stop image-name
docker rm image-name
docker run --name image-name [OPTIONS] docker-registry/image-name [COMMAND] [ARG...]
```

What we have done in the above code is pull the container, stop the running one and then remove it. We can then run the new image.

Chapter 5- Networking in Docker

After starting the Docker, a virtual interface is created on the machine and given the name *"dockero"*. The Docker then finds an IP address and a corresponding subnet mask, which it then assigns to this interface. Note that the IP address is picked from the specified range of private IP addresses.

There are numerous networking commands which can be run on the Docker terminal. Some of these can only be run once the Docker is started and they cannot be changed as it runs.

Suppose that you have built a new bridge in Ubuntu. The Docker can be configured as follows so as to recognize this bridge:

Open the file *"/etc/default/docker"* and edit it as follows:

```
$ echo 'DOCKER_OPTS="-b=bridge0"' >> /etc/default/docker
```

After that, use the following command so as to restart the Docker server:

```
$ sudo service docker start
```

DNS Configuration

The DNS (Domain Name Server) is responsible for resolving host names to IP addresses. The Docker should supply each of the containers with DNS configuration and a Host name. Open the container terminal and then run the *"mount"* command. You will observe the following output:

```
$$ mount
...
/dev/disk/by-uuid/1fec...ebdf on /etc/hostname type ext4 ...
/dev/disk/by-uuid/1fec...ebdf on /etc/hosts type ext4 ...
/dev/disk/by-uuid/1fec...ebdf on /etc/resolv.conf type ext4 ...
```

The output shows the three *"/etc"* files in the system.

Container communication

It is possible for containers to communicate with each other. However, each of the host machines should be willing and ready to forward the IP packets. The parameter *"ip_forward"* determines this. For packets to be passed between containers, the value of this parameter should be set to 1. The Docker server should be left at its default setting, that is, *"--ip-forward=true"*. The Docker will then set the parameter *"ip_forward"* to 1. If you need to check the value of this setting, run the following commands:

```
$ sysctl net.ipv4.conf.all.forwarding
net.ipv4.conf.all.forwarding = 0
$ sysctl net.ipv4.conf.all.forwarding=1
$ sysctl net.ipv4.conf.all.forwarding
net.ipv4.conf.all.forwarding = 1
```

It is the wish of most Docker users to have the parameter *"ip_forward"* set to 1 so that communication between containers can be made possible.

You also need to be aware of the Docker *"iptables"*. If you set the parameter *"iptables"* to false, the Docker will not change the settings once the daemon is started. This feature can be used to restrict how a certain container is accessed. In this case, a negated rule should be added to the top of the Docker filter chain. Consider the figure given below:

```
$ iptables -I DOCKER -i ext_if ! -s 8.8.8.8 -j DROP
```

With the above command, only the external IP source of 8.8.8.8 will be able to access the containers. Consider the command given below:

```
$ sudo iptables -L -n
. . .
Chain FORWARD (policy ACCEPT)
target     prot opt source                destination
DOCKER     all  --  0.0.0.0/0             0.0.0.0/0
DROP       all  --  0.0.0.0/0             0.0.0.0/0
. . .
```

The command helps us to check the default policy setting of the parameter "*iptables*", which can either be "*ACCEPT*" or "*DROP*".

Note that with Docker containers, connection to the outside world can be made but the opposite is not true. For each of the outgoing connections, this will appear as if its source is one of the IP addresses of the host machine. This is shown in the figure given below:

```
$ sudo iptables -t nat -L -n
...
Chain POSTROUTING (policy ACCEPT)
target       prot opt source              destination
MASQUERADE  all  --  172.17.0.0/16        0.0.0.0/0
```

However, it is possible that you might want your container to accept any connections which are incoming. This is in contrast to the default setting. If this is the case, then you have to provide some options when running the *"docker run"* command. The *"-p"* or the *"--publish-all=true|false"* option can be supplied to the command. Each of the Docker ports will then be identified with an *"EXPOSE"* line.

By examining the NAT (Network Address Translation) table, you can know whatever has been done by the Docker to your system. This is shown below:

```
# What your NAT rules might look like when Docker
# is finished setting up a -P forward:

$ iptables -t nat -L -n
...
Chain DOCKER (2 references)
target     prot opt source              destination
DNAT       tcp -- 0.0.0.0/0             0.0.0.0/0        tcp dpt:49153 to:172.17.0.2:8

# What your NAT rules might look like when Docker
# is finished setting up a -p 80:80 forward:

Chain DOCKER (2 references)
target     prot opt source              destination
DNAT       tcp -- 0.0.0.0/0             0.0.0.0/0        tcp dpt:80 to:172.17.0.2:80
```

IPV6 in the Docker

The Docker container is default configured to IPV4 by the Docker server. If you need to enable the IPV4/IPV6 dualstack support in your system, use the "—*ipv6*" flag when running the Docker daemon. With this, the bridge "*dockero*" will be set up with the IPV6 address "*fe80::1*", which is link-local.

If the container has already been created, then it will only get the IPV6 link-local address by default. If you need to have globally routable IPV6 addresses for your container, then you have to specify a subnet for the IPV6 from which the addresses will be picked. This can be set as follows as we start the Docker daemon:

```
docker -d --ipv6 --fixed-cidr-v6="2001:db8:1::/64"
```

Subnets for Docker containers should have a minimum size of /80. This is of great importance as it prevents the invalidation of the cache.

If the parameter "--*fixed-cidr-v6*" is set, then a new route will be added to the routing table by the Docker.

```
$ ip -6 route add 2001:db8:1::/64 dev docker0

$ sysctl net.ipv6.conf.default.forwarding=1

$ sysctl net.ipv6.conf.all.forwarding=1
```

Chapter 6- Docker Orchestration

There is a need for us to orchestrate the distributed apps for the Docker. Most of the tools which can be used for this purpose have been released but are not ready for use in a production environment. In this chapter, we will discuss the Docker Machine Beta, which is one of the tools that can be used for this purpose.

Docker Machine Beta

With this tool, one can move from zero to Docker. The tool is able to create a Docker engine on your computer, in your data center and cloud providers. You can then configure the Docker client to talk to these. It is used as follows:

```
$ docker-machine create -d virtualbox dev
[info] Downloading boot2docker...
[info] Creating SSH key...
[info] Creating VirtualBox VM...
[info] Starting VirtualBox VM...
[info] Waiting for VM to start...
[info] "dev" has been created and is now the active machine.
[info] To point your Docker client at it, run this in your shell: $(docker-machine env dev)
```

As shown in the above figure, the process is verbal as it tells us how it is progressing and what it is doing. After that, run the following command:

```
$ $(docker-machine env dev)
```

After the above command, you will be set, and in a position to verify the installation and setup. This can be done by running the "*hello world*" example as shown below:

```
$ docker run busybox echo hello world
Unable to find image 'busybox' locally
Pulling repository busybox
e72ac664f4f0: Download complete
511136ea3c5a: Download complete
df7546f9f060: Download complete
e433a6c5b276: Download complete
hello world
```

This tool supports the following providers:

- VMware vSphere

- OpenStack

- VMware Fusion

- SoftLayer

- Microsoft Azure

- VirtualBox

- DigitalOcean

- Google Compute Engine

- Microsoft Hyper-V

- Rackspace

- VMware vCloud Air

- Amazon EC2

The Docker Compose

With this tool, you can easily spin up the multi-container applications. It lets you define the components of your application, their volumes, containers, links, configurations and others in a unit file. You can then use a single command to set up everything which is necessary for your application to run. It is closely related to Fig, so if you are good with that, all the better. To use Compose on your system, there are three steps that you need to follow.

First, you need to begin by defining the environment for your application by use of a Dockerfile, so that it can be able to run anywhere. This is shown in the figure given below:

```
FROM python:2.7
WORKDIR /code
ADD requirements.txt /code/
RUN pip install -r requirements.txt
ADD . /code
CMD python app.py
```

The next step involves the definition of the components which make up your application. This can be done in the file "*docker-compose.yml*" and these components will be in a position to run together and in an environment which is isolated. This is shown below:

```
web:
   build: .
   links:
      - redis
   ports:
      - "5000:5000"
 redis:
    image: redis
```

Lastly, you need to run the following command:

```
docker-compose up
```

What the above command does is run your entire application, and the order in which the components are to be started is established.

Chapter 7- Docker Security

In the Docker, security is highly important. The security of the kernel needs to be considered very much. The Docker daemon itself can also become compromised if security is not well handled. Loopholes can also exist in the configuration file of the container, either by default or once the users have made some configurations.

We explored the *"docker"* group in our previous chapters. For the sake of the security of the Docker, be careful about the kind of users that you add to this group, as they can be a threat to the security of the system. Any use added to this group becomes a root use of the Docker.

To ensure the security of file systems, the Docker will have made some mount points read only. These include the following:

- /sys
- /proc/sys
- /proc/sysrq-trigger
- /proc/irq
- /proc/bus

If "*CAP_SYS_ADMIN*" is removed from containers, then the execution of syscall or the modification of namespaces by processes will be prevented. Our intention is to avoid the processes of the container from mounting file systems or remounting the file systems which are read-only.

```
--cap-add --cap-drop
```

With the Docker, it is possible for us to do an adjustment on the capabilities of the Docker. This means that you can remove the capabilities which the container does not need. Suppose that your container is not in need of "*setgid*" and "*setuid*". These can be removed by executing the following command:

```
docker run --cap-drop setuid --cap-drop setgid -ti rhel7 /bin/sh
```

The following is the case when you are running Red Hat Enterprise Linux in your system. If you need to add or remove all of the capabilities, then run the following command:

```
docker run --cap-add all --cap-drop sys-admin -ti rhel7 /bin/sh
```

With the above command, all the capabilities except the "*sys-admin*" capability will be added. If the security of the Docker is ensured, then the entire better, since all of the components will have been safeguarded.

Conclusion

It can be concluded the Docker is a very important project. You should begin by understanding its basics, which we learned in the first part of this book. If you have not read that part of the book, kindly consider doing so. The Docker is solely based on features which are related to Linux. This is why we natively install it on Linux. However, there are versions of different distributions of the Linux OS which can support the Docker, while other versions of the same cannot support the Docker.

It is good for you to know the versions that are supported, depending on the distribution of the Linux you are using. In Mac OS X and Windows operating systems, we used the Boot2Docker for the purpose of installation of the Docker. This installs the Docker itself, the virtual machine and the Boot2Docker management tool in the system. Without this, we cannot run the Docker in these operating system.

However, this is not the case in Linux. In this case, the Docker can be directly installed into the OS and then we begin to use it. The Docker is largely used in production environments. Note that there are certain distributions of Linux which are used in commercial environments, while others cannot be. Some of these include the Oracle Linux, red Hat Enterprise Linux, SUSE Enterprise Linux and others.

This is why you need to know how to install the Docker in these operating systems. After the installation process completes, you need to test whether it succeeded or failed. This is because you should be cautious with production environments, as a minor error can lead to huge losses. However, there are security tools for the Docker which have been introduced.

These have been discussed in this book and you need to know how to use them. The Docker can also be used for the purpose of networking. However, you need to know that it is able to establish connections to the outside world, but not allow them in.

Other Books from Matthew Gimson

ANDROID PROGRAMMING: Complete Introduction for Beginners -Step By Step Guide How to Create Your Own Android App Easy!

ANDROID GAME PROGRAMMING: COMPLETE INTRODUCTION FOR BEGINNERS: STEP BY STEP GUIDE HOW TO CREATE YOUR OWN ANDROID APP EASY!

**Linux Command Line: FAST and EASY!
(Linux Commands, Bash Scripting
Tricks, Linux Shell Programming Tips
and Bash One-Liners)**

Linux Command Line: Become a Linux Expert! (Input/Output Redirection, Wildcards, File Security, Processes Managing, Shell Programming Advanced Features, GUI elements, Useful Linux Commands)

PHP and MySQL Programming for Beginners: A Step by Step Course From Zero to Professional

Python Programming: Getting started FAST With Learning of Python Programming Basics in No Time.

DOCKER: Everything You Need to Know to Master Docker (Docker Containers, Linking Containers, Whalesay Image, Docker Installing on Mac OS X and Windows OS)

Docker: Docker Guide for Production Environment (Programming is Easy Book 8)

Excel VBA Programming: Learn Excel VBA Programming FAST and EASY! (Programming is Easy Book 9)

VAGRANT: Make Your Life Easier With VAGRANT. Master VAGRANT FAST and EASY! (Programming is Easy Book 10)

SCALA PROGRAMMING: Learn Scala Programming FAST and EASY! (Programming is Easy Book 11)

NODE. JS: Practical Guide for Beginners (Programming is Easy Book 12)

IOS 8 APP DEVELOPMENT. Develop Your Own App FAST and EASY!

www.ingramcontent.com/pod-product-compliance
Lightning Source LLC
Chambersburg PA
CBHW051342170526
45166CB00002B/924